ATTACKING ABSENTEEISM

Lynn Tylczak

CRISP PUBLICATIONS, INC.
Los Altos, California

ATTACKING ABSENTEEISM

Lynn Tylczak

CREDITS
Editor: **Tony Hicks**
Designer: **Carol Harris**
Typesetting: **Interface Studio**
Cover Design: **Carol Harris**
Artwork: **Ralph Mapson**

Copyright © 1990 by Crisp Publications, Inc.
Printed in the United States of America

Crisp books are distributed in Canada by Reid Publishing, Ltd., P.O. Box 7267, Oakville, Ontario, Canada L6J 6L6.

In Australia by Career Builders, P.O. Box 1051, Springwood, Brisbane, Queensland, Australia 4127.

And in New Zealand by Career Builders, P.O. Box 571, Manurewa, New Zealand.

Library of Congress Catalog Card Number 90-80078
Tylczak, Lynn
Attacking Absenteeism
ISBN 1-56052-042-6

PREFACE

This self-study book will help you attack—and push back—absenteeism.

Surprisingly, some of the most effective strategies for combating absenteeism are inexpensive and easy to administer. Many can simply be overlaid onto existing programs. No muss, no fuss, but a big plus.

The objectives of this book are to

- demonstrate the problems and parameters of absenteeism.

- show you how to create an environment conducive to excellent attendance.

- give you step-by-step procedures to slash absenteeism (NOTE: Many of these suggestions can be used on a departmental basis without top management involvement.

- document what the effective use of proper policies can do.

You don't have to have an absentee problem. You can have an absentee solution. This book will show you how. Good Luck!

Lynn Tylczak

Lynn Tylczak

CONTENTS

(Continued next page)

CONTENTS (Continued)

INTRODUCTION

Is your department, division or organization suffering from terminal absenteeism? It's an illness that strikes nearly every business, leaving it weak at the margins and down in the mouth.

Absenteeism claims

- 3.2 percent of all scheduled work hours
- 90 million hours per week
- 416 million workdays per year
- 9 days lost per employee per year
- 1 employee in every 15 on a weekly basis

Absentee costs are difficult to quantify. Experts estimate direct wage loses of more than $30 billion per year, and that's just the beginning. Employers also need to consider the costs of supplementary or replacement workers. These costs include:

Regular wages, overtime wages, and company benefits
Supplementary benefits, such as Social Security, worker's compensation, and unemployment compensation
Administration of recruitment, selection orientation, and training
Penalty costs resulting from delays

Absenteeism also has less tangible costs. It forces managers to deal with problems of morale, discipline, job dissatisfaction, job stress, team spirit, productivity, turnover, production quality, additional administration and overhead.

To summarize: You don't just have an absentee problem. You have a profit problem. But don't feel *too* down—in the time it takes to complete this book, things will be looking up!

P A R T 1

THE PROBLEM WITH ABSENTEEISM

ABSENTEE PROBLEM #1: CAMOUFLAGE

Keeping track of employees who aren't on the job is practically a full-time job. The May and Baker Company, for example, has 34 categories of time loss:

HOLIDAY AND SICKNESS REASONS

Annual Leave
Work-related accidents or diseases
Certified sickness (other than work-related accidents or diseases)
Self-certified sickness
Appointment with dentist, optician, chiropractor
Doctor's surgery appointment
Hospital appointment
Antenatal appointment

EDUCATION AND TRAINING

Day release
Study leave
Examination leave
Off-the-job training in the company
Out-of-company training

EMPLOYEE RELATIONS

Suspension with pay
Suspension without pay
Strike
Secondary industrial action
Layoff
Short time
Being stood off
Union duties (as union rep)
Union duties (as union member)

SOCIAL, COMMUNITY, AND OTHER REASONS

Civic duties
Jury services
Military reserve
Preretirement reduced working
Marriage leave
Bereavement leave
Compassionate leave
Lieu day
Rest day
Unauthorized absence
Unknown reasons for absence

The problem is obvious. How does a manager quantify and deal with an absentee problem when it hides among legitimate leaves?

ABSENTEE PROBLEM #2:
EMPLOYEE ATTITUDES

Cavalier employee attitudes result in a cavalcade of excuses. Consider these actual, but out-of-this-world, excuses collected by Robert Half International, the well-known recruiting firm.

• My dog hid my toupee in the basement.

• I didn't get any sleep the last couple of nights because I stayed up looking for Halley's comet.

• As a joke my six-year-old son set all the clocks back an hour.

• Someone stole one of my shoes on the bus.

• I had to take my grandfather to the baseball game.

• My astrologer warned me not to come to work before noon on Wednesday.

• I was late getting back from my ski weekend because it snowed so much the roads were closed.

• I ate so much on vacation that none of my clothes fit. So I spent the morning having them altered.

• I was late because my digital watch blew a chip.

• My spouse forgot where our car was parked coming home from the office party.

• My parakeet spoke for the first time and I waited for him to do it again so I could tape record it.

• When you work as hard as I do, you're entitled to a day off now and then.

It is difficult to solve a serious problem when employees don't take it seriously.

ABSENTEE PROBLEM #3: SYSTEMS THAT ENCOURAGE, RATHER THAN DISCOURAGE, ABSENTEEISM

Does your company have an anti-attendance policy? General Motors used to. Here's how it worked.

Employee benefits were not adjusted to reflect absenteeism. Workers were making $10 an hour in direct wages, plus $230 a week in benefits. As a result:

- Workers with a perfect attendance record for the week earned $15.75 per hour ($400 in wages plus $230 in benefits divided by 40 hours).

- Workers who missed a day earned $17.19 per hour ($320 in wages plus $230 in benefits divided by 32 hours).

- Workers who missed three days earned $19.58 per hour ($240 in wages plus $230 in benefits divided by 16 hours).

Is it any wonder that GM's controllable absenteeism ("hooky") rate was around 11 percent?

A GM union steward once asked a young and healthy female employee why she had such an abysmal absentee record.

Her response: "My husband's fringe benefits don't cover our needs, and we can also use a little extra income. We don't need the full $400 a week (of salary), and I want to spend some time with my children."

Talk about role reversal! This employee was working for benefits, not for pay. To her, *pay* was a benefit. And so was a system that paid benefits to employees without making them pay their dues.

ABSENTEE PROBLEM #4:
COMPLEX CAUSES

Many causes affect absenteeism. Researchers have compiled quite a list of
influences, some good and some bad. Consider the following:

- Employee Specifics

  Gender roles and responsibilities, age, financial status, family activities,
  personal illness (including abuse of alcohol or drugs), the desire to spend time
  with friends, family functions, personal business, unavailability of child care,
  family illness, the desire for more leisure time, education, a second job, hobbies
  (e.g., disappears the first day of the hunting season!), house maintenance

- Emotional and Psychological Concerns

  The desire to break from routine, the level of morale, the employee's value
  system, strength of the work ethic, self-image, self-growth needs, job stress,
  personal commitment to the job, social or psychological withdrawal, job
  dissatisfaction, lack of acceptance by peers, peer pressure

- Financial Concerns

  Loss of wages, disciplinary time off, loss of promotional or wage-raise
  opportunities, loss of job, loss of benefits

ABSENTEE PROBLEM #4:
COMPLEX CAUSES (Continued)

- Job and Company Specifies

  Tenure, work status, job responsibilities, a desire to get away from coworkers, a desire to get away from the supervisor, disciplinary talk, union or nonunion shop, union strength, loss of production, disciplinary probation, fault or no-fault absentee program, job involvement, employer commitment, incentive program, workgroup size, job range or scope, workgroup norms, job variety, job autonomy, task significance, worker participation in decision making, distributive justice, pay equity, leadership style, supervisor's attitude toward absenteeism, job specialization, work communications, paid sick leave, amount of paid vacation, size of firm, type of firm (manufacturing or service)

- Miscellaneous

  Car pool, cost of transportation, lack of transportation, right-to-work laws, local and national unemployment rate, geographic area

If a manager has 20 employees subject to these 74 factors that influence absenteeism, how many absentee problems does the manager have? Twenty, one for each employee? Seventy-four, one for each influence? No such luck. Every employee is touched by every influence in one way or another, so the manager has 1480 absentee problems (20 employees times 74 influences).

How can this manager hope to cope with so complex a problem?

ABSENTEE PROBLEM #5: THE GOOD, THE BAD, AND THE CONFUSED

Knowing what affects absenteeism isn't the same as knowing *what effects* to expect. Consider the following:

• Do union shops have a higher absentee rate than their nonunion counterparts? Here's what the experts say:

> Position one: Absolutely. Union shops have a higher level of job dissatisfaction (a major cause of absenteeism), more paid-absence programs, greater employee security, and better grievance procedures following a related job loss.

> Position two: Absolutely not. Unions press for justice and equality, lessening job dissatisfaction. Better vacation plans encourage legitimate leaves. Unions and employees with good work records don't want to carry repeat offenders.

Experts agree that having a union affects absenteeism. They just don't agree on whether the effect is positive or negative!

• Do women have a higher absentee rate than the opposite sex? Well...

> Against the tender gender: Absolutely. Check virtually any major study on the subject. The statistics speak for themselves.

> Gender defenders: Of course women have a higher absentee rate. They are more likely to be employed in low-pay, low-morale jobs. The problem is the job, not the gender.

Gender is an influence on absenteeism, but it isn't *the* influence.

To quote one absentee expert: ''We know all the ingredients that go into an absenteeism problem. We just haven't figured out the recipe.''

ABSENTEE PROBLEM #6: TAKING THE ABSENTEE PROBLEM TOO SERIOUSLY.

Go ahead, read the title again. It isn't a typo.

Ironically, taking the absentee problem too seriously can create more trouble than it solves. For example:

SITUATION 1: Is your absenteeism program so strict that employees end up on the job when they should be on their backs?

- An individual continues (or returns) to work while ill or injured, exposing others to illness or a greater probability of an on-the-job injury.

- An individual works instead of dealing with other crucial obligations, personal or social. The distraction and stress eventually lead to a serious illness or injury.

- An individual needs R&R, but refuses to go AWOL (Absent With Obvious Legitimacy). His or her productivity slumps, and the individual eventually breaks under the fatigue.

An ounce of preventative absenteeism is worth a pound of, well ... curative absenteeism!

SITUATION 2: Is your strict absentee program equitable—but less than fair?

- Like clockwork, Jim misses one day a month. It is invariably a Friday or a Monday. He never calls in, never gives any warning.

- Brenda missed 12 days of work last year following a serious operation that was scheduled three months in advance of the absence.

Both Jim and Brenda missed the same amount of work. Should they be tarred and feathered with the same brush? Probably not.

SUMMARY

It's always darkest before the dawn of a new idea. As we've seen, absenteeism is a real problem. It costs businesses billions of dollars and trillions of heartaches. Absenteeism is influenced by dozens of interrelated factors and exacerbated by business systems that reward—rather than retard—the problem. In short, it is difficult to quantify, qualify, or rectify.

Difficult, but not impossible. New philosophies, programs, and procedures are helping businesses slash their absentee rates by up to 50 percent.

Interested? It's your turn to turn the tables on absenteeism.

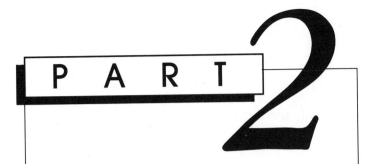

PART 2

GET WITH THE PROGRAM!

THE PERFECT ABSENTEEISM PROGRAM

Sorry, there isn't one. That is, there isn't *one* absentee program that works best for *all* businesses. A program that works well for highly skilled professionals, for example, may be totally ineffective for less skilled hamburger helpers.

However, there are some basic rules for designing *your* perfect absentee program.* Experts call them the Ten Commandments of Absenteeism. You might call them the golden rules: They offer a golden opportunity to improve absentee rates and increase profits.

Some of these suggestions improve the work environment. Others develop supervisory skills and support systems. One affects pay. All will reduce absenteeism. Follow a majority of them and your track record should show significant if not dramatic improvement.

---

*Not all of the rules will apply to your business. If they did, there would be one perfect absentee plan!

THE TEN COMMANDMENTS OF ABSENTEEISM

1. Thou shalt measure and track absenteeism.

2. Thou shalt discuss absentee issues with employees.

3. Thou shalt tie compensation to work hours.

4. Thou shalt help employees maintain or improve their attendance records.

5. Thou shalt reward good attendance records.

6. Thou shalt utilize fair and justifiable discipline.

7. Thou shalt carefully match employees to jobs and careers.

8. Thou shalt promote safety and health.

9. Thou shalt train supervisors to support—rather than abort—the absentee program.

10. Thou shalt fine-tune the absentee program to meet specific company needs.

Putting these golden rules to work for your company doesn't require the Midas touch. Often, all you need is some touch-up work on your current absentee program.

PART 3

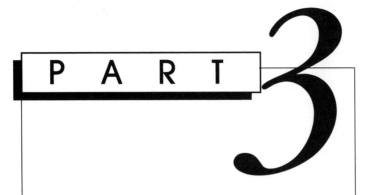

INTRODUCTION TO ORGANIZATION

ORGANIZATIONAL PROBLEMS

Does the company facilitate—or debilitate—your attempts to decrease absenteeism? Do you subconsciously do the same?

These are legitimate questions. Why? Because:

- Companies don't hire homogenous humans. Positions, and personnel, differ. Policies and techniques that greatly influence a career engineer may not affect a ''go-fer'' loafer. If your policies and techniques are in keeping with your people, keep them up.

- Situations may change faster than policies. Many of us refuse to adapt current programs until we have the benefit of 20/20 hindsight. In the meantime, we see absentee rates rise . . .

- Anti-absentee attempts may be based on incorrect assumptions. On-site day care probably won't reduce absenteeism if the average employee age is 57. Peer pressure won't work if there is no peer fear or cohort support.

- Actions may speak louder than words. Absentee managers are role models for absentee employees.

Don't be frustrated if you find that absenteeism gets more support than the absentee program. Help is available.

THIS WAY FOR HELP

ORGANIZING THE ORGANIZATION

If you haven't been utilizing the absentee golden rules, don't worry. These ''gilt ridden'' methods of control have been used with varying levels of success. (success depends on how applicable and appropriate the method is to the specific situation. These methods of control are listed roughly in decreasing order of effectiveness.) Which do you do? Or might you do?

	Seldom	Once in Awhile	Always	Will Consider
1. Employees talk to me when they call in absent.	☐	☐	☐	☐
2. I terminate employees with excessive absenteeism.	☐	☐	☐	☐
3. Benefits reflect hours worked.	☐	☐	☐	☐
4. Progressive disciplinary schedules are used.	☐	☐	☐	☐
5. I identify, discipline, and focus my attention on chronic absentee abusers.	☐	☐	☐	☐
6. I separate excused and unexcused absences and treat them accordingly.	☐	☐	☐	☐
7. I make a note of my employees' absentee rates during their performance appraisals.	☐	☐	☐	☐
8. I apply the absentee program with uniformity.	☐	☐	☐	☐
9. I have new employees read the absentee policy, ask questions if necessary, and initial it for their files.	☐	☐	☐	☐
10. I show employees how much money our profit center loses each month as a result of absenteeism. I demonstrate how these losses will affect bonuses, raises, and benefits.	☐	☐	☐	☐

(Continued next page)

ORGANIZING THE ORGANIZATION (Continued)

	Seldom	Once in Awhile	Always	Will Consider
11. I require employees to get a doctor's excuse for medical absences.	☐	☐	☐	☐
12. I assign ''points'' for each absence, giving increased weight to unexcused or suspect absences.	☐	☐	☐	☐
13. I discuss the absentee program during meetings, and worker orientations.	☐	☐	☐	☐
14. I maintain daily attendance records.	☐	☐	☐	☐
15. I make past work attendance a consideration during preemployment screening.	☐	☐	☐	☐
16. I use a no-fault absentee plan (see the case studies in Part 6).	☐	☐	☐	☐
17. I analyze my daily attendance records on a monthly basis and provide feedback to employees.	☐	☐	☐	☐
18. I encourage employees to schedule appointments before or after work, on days off, or during lunch breaks. I give less weight to absentee appointments when the employee also commits some of her free time.	☐	☐	☐	☐
19. To enhance peer group pressure, I require employees to fill in for missing team members.	☐	☐	☐	☐
20. I use well pay, rather than sick pay, procedures (see the case studies in Part 6).	☐	☐	☐	☐

ORGANIZING THE ORGANIZATION
(Continued)

	Seldom	Once in Awhile	Always	Will Consider
21. The personnel department maintains daily attendance records in addition to my own.	☐	☐	☐	☐
22. I allow employees to amend their past attendance record by maintaining subsequent good attendance.	☐	☐	☐	☐
23. I actively practice absentee control—it is a conscious effort.	☐	☐	☐	☐
24. I conduct a formal employee interview after every absence.	☐	☐	☐	☐
25. My employees can work on flextime.	☐	☐	☐	☐
26. I recognize good employee attendance records.	☐	☐	☐	☐
27. I encourage employees to take advantage of the company's substance abuse program.	☐	☐	☐	☐
28. I issue financial bonuses for good attendance.	☐	☐	☐	☐
29. My boss asks me about departmental attendance during my own appraisals.	☐	☐	☐	☐
30. I check up on missing employees with a visit or phone call to their residence.	☐	☐	☐	☐
31. I promote job enrichment and enlargement and job rotation.	☐	☐	☐	☐

ORGANIZING THE ORGANIZATION
(Continued)

	Seldom	Once in Awhile	Always	Will Consider
32. I actively remind workers about our company health, diet and home safety programs, and fitness plan.	☐	☐	☐	☐
33. I've developed an ''absence bank,'' which allows employees to add ''unused'' absence days to their scheduled vacations.	☐	☐	☐	☐
34. We have an attendance lottery or other contest.	☐	☐	☐	☐
35. I encourage local doctors and dentists to offer Saturday appointments.	☐	☐	☐	☐
36. The company offers on-site day-care centers or other day-care support.	☐	☐	☐	☐
37. I send a letter to employees' spouses that documents earnings, bonuses, and promotions lost because of excessive absenteeism.	☐	☐	☐	☐

SUMMARY

There is one *caveat emptor:* think before you buy into any wholesale change for your absentee policy. Ask these basic who, what, when, where, why, and how questions for every proposed change:

WHO

Who will be affected by this change? Who will gain or lose? _____

_____

_____

Who will help implement or administer this change? _____

_____

_____

Who needs to be consulted? _____

_____

_____

Who specifically needs to be sold on the ideas of change (for example, an employee who has a lot of political clout with his peers)?

_____

_____

Who can document the need to change? _____

_____

_____

Who has gone through similar changes (and with what result)? _____

_____

_____

WHAT, WHEN, WHY AND HOW AHEAD

SUMMARY (Continued)

WHAT

What organizational change is the most appropriate? _____
_____
_____

What are the potential advantages? Disadvantages? _____
_____
_____

What is the downside risk? _____
_____
_____

What needs to be done to implement the change? _____
_____
_____

What organizational components will (or could) be affected? _____
_____
_____

What will this change cost—directly and indirectly? _____
_____
_____

WHEN

When do we discuss this potential change with employees? Managers? Staff?
_____
_____

When can we make this change? _____
_____
_____

When will we evaluate our program and make any necessary change?
_____
_____

When—under what circumstances—should we consider another change?
_____
_____

SUMMARY (Continued)

WHERE

Where do we first implement the change? In a particular department?
In a particular facility? Everywhere?

_____

_____

Where do we introduce the change—corporate newsletter? Small departmental
meetings? Management retreat?

_____

_____

WHY

Why should we make any change? _____

_____

_____

Why should we make this change? _____

_____

_____

Why not revise—rather than scrap—the status quo? _____

_____

_____

Why would anybody be against this change: managers, workers, staff?

_____

_____

Why do we think this would solve our problem(s)? _____

_____

_____

SUMMARY (Continued)

HOW

How do we implement the change? _____
_____
_____

How can we adapt generalized ideas to meet our specific needs? _____
_____
_____

How do we integrate the new program into our old ways? _____
_____
_____

How do we minimize any downside risks or disadvantages? _____
_____
_____

How do we expand or add advantages? _____
_____
_____

How do we make the change a positive experience for our people? _____
_____
_____

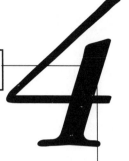

PART

JOIN THE MORALE MAJORITY

JOIN THE MORALE MAJORITY

THE EIGHT STEPS

High employee morale is key to a low absentee rate. There are eight steps to improving employee moral:

Step One: **Emulate**

Step Two: **Appreciate**

Step Three: **Ingratiate**

Step Four: **Stimulate**

Step Five: **Integrate**

Step Six: **Initiate**

Step Seven: **Contemplate**

Step Eight: **Delegate**

The following pages dissect these ''ate'' steps in detail. Fill in the forms. Every ''Always'' is a plus, every ''Seldom'' represents the opportunity to improve. Identify where you stand now and what steps you need to take. Think of the ''ate'' steps in terms of their behavior ingredients. That way you won't bite off more than you can chew.

Step One: **Emulate**

Look at your own attendance behavior. Is it praiseworthy or questionable? The following checklist (answered honestly) will separate those setting a positive example from those who need to clean up their act.

	Seldom	Once in Awhile	Always	Will Consider
1. I get to work on time—or better yet, early.	☐	☐	☐	☐
2. I come back from lunch or breaks on time or early.	☐	☐	☐	☐
3. I am one of the last out the door at quitting time.	☐	☐	☐	☐
4. I schedule my absences well in advance.	☐	☐	☐	☐
5. My office staff and crew always know where I am (at least one person is instructed to tell those who need to know where I am at all times).	☐	☐	☐	☐
6. I work at the office—rather than at home—during regular work hours.	☐	☐	☐	☐
7. If I occassionally work at home during regular office hours, I encourage people to call me and I make regular calls to the office.	☐	☐	☐	☐
8. I use the same work reporting system as my crew (time card, punch clock, etc.).	☐	☐	☐	☐
9. I park my car where it can attest to my presence.	☐	☐	☐	☐
10. I keep my office door open so that people know I am in there working.	☐	☐	☐	☐
11. I am there when my crew needs to work overtime.	☐	☐	☐	☐
12. I apply the absentee rules equitably and fairly to everyone.	☐	☐	☐	☐

Step Two: **Appreciate**

You catch more flies with honey than you do with vinegar. If you want employees to improve their absentee records, you need to sound like a broken record giving positive feedback, positive feedback, positive feedback . . .

Assess your feedback faculties:

When it comes to reducing absenteeism:	Seldom	Once in Awhile	Always	Will Consider
1. I always offer positive reinforcement.	☐	☐	☐	☐
2. I give verbal encouragement.	☐	☐	☐	☐
3. I use visual reinforcement, such as signs, and congratulatory flyers.	☐	☐	☐	☐
4. I reward good absentee records (e.g., first choice of vacation times).	☐	☐	☐	☐
5. I address absentee issues in a positive way.	☐	☐	☐	☐
6. I generate top management support for absentee issues.	☐	☐	☐	☐
7. I generate employee peer support for absentee issues.	☐	☐	☐	☐
8. I acknowledge individual success—both ongoing success and improvement.	☐	☐	☐	☐
9. I acknowledge group success and improvement.	☐	☐	☐	☐
10. My appreciation is honest.	☐	☐	☐	☐
11. I recognize all improvements no matter how small.	☐	☐	☐	☐
12. I stress future improvements rather than past problems.	☐	☐	☐	☐

Step Three: **Ingratiate**

To economists, the law of supply and demand means that the free market supplies what consumers demand. To managers, the law of supply and demand means that no matter how much respect and loyalty managers demand, their subordinates are under no legal obligation to supply it.

Managers must command—rather than demand—respect. This checklist will offer guidance on how to go about it. Aim for the always!

	Seldom	Once in Awhile	Always	Will Consider
1. I am fair with my employees.	☐	☐	☐	☐
2. I try to be impartial toward employees.	☐	☐	☐	☐
3. I stress consistency in dealing with employees.	☐	☐	☐	☐
4. I am up-front in my communications and actions.	☐	☐	☐	☐
5. I am a part of the team— though team members recognize that I am not a peer.	☐	☐	☐	☐
6. I only make promises that I know I can keep.	☐	☐	☐	☐
7. I admit my imperfections.	☐	☐	☐	☐
8. When I am wrong, I apologize.	☐	☐	☐	☐
9. I acknowledge the importance of my employees—as individuals and as members of the team.	☐	☐	☐	☐
10. I am loyal to my employees.	☐	☐	☐	☐
11. I acknowledge that my major role as a manager is to facilitate the work of my subordinates.	☐	☐	☐	☐
12. I do unto my workers as I would want my workers to do unto me.	☐	☐	☐	☐
13. I acknowledge not having all the answers.	☐	☐	☐	☐
14. I LISTEN.	☐	☐	☐	☐

Step Four: **Stimulate**

Everybody needs a break once in a while. If you break up the routine of work, you put the brakes on absenteeism.

Give your employees the break job they need.

	Seldom	Once in Awhile	Always	Will Consider
1. I challenge my employees with tasks, ideas, and suggestions.	☐	☐	☐	☐
2. I encourage employees to challenge the status quo.	☐	☐	☐	☐
3. I always try to offer something new and exciting (instead of new and threatening!).	☐	☐	☐	☐
4. I schedule interesting things on otherwise uninteresting days.	☐	☐	☐	☐
5. I plan surprises.	☐	☐	☐	☐
6. I keep track of, and acknowledge, unusual items.	☐	☐	☐	☐
7. I encourage positive competition.	☐	☐	☐	☐
8. I challenge employees to redefine themselves, their work roles, and the team.	☐	☐	☐	☐
9. I support employee ambitions, goals, and dreams.	☐	☐	☐	☐
10. I provide cross training.	☐	☐	☐	☐
11. I match employees to potential mentors.	☐	☐	☐	☐
12. I am a terminal cheer leader.	☐	☐	☐	☐
13. I provide "cliffhangers."	☐	☐	☐	☐
14. I don't let the physical work environment get stagnant.	☐	☐	☐	☐
15. I avoid overstimulation and change for the sake of change.	☐	☐	☐	☐

Step Five: Integrate

Are you part of the problem or part of the solution? That depends. Do your employees feel like part of the company or part of the inventory? Are you a part of the team or apart from the team? Let's find out.

	Seldom	Once in Awhile	Always	Will Consider
1. I keep my employees informed of what is going on in the department and the company.	☐	☐	☐	☐
2. I encourage healthy interdepartmental competitions (and I do my best to help my team win!).	☐	☐	☐	☐
3. My personal objectives are in sync with team objectives.	☐	☐	☐	☐
4. I respect other team members' input and ideas.	☐	☐	☐	☐
5. When I disagree with other team members I do it as a team player, not as a boss.	☐	☐	☐	☐
6. I try to pair employees whose chemistry, personalities, temperaments, attitudes, or abilities mesh.	☐	☐	☐	☐
7. I help my employees master team skills.	☐	☐	☐	☐
8. I reward and acknowledge group accomplishments.	☐	☐	☐	☐
9. I credit the team—rather than myself—for group successes.	☐	☐	☐	☐
10. I have a realistic and constructive approach toward group conflicts and attitudes.	☐	☐	☐	☐
11. I encourage healthy communication, and discourage bickering.	☐	☐	☐	☐

Step Six: **Initiate**

Do you follow the leader or lead the followers? If you want lower absentee rates, you need to actively promote worker participation. You need to consider the following steps:

	Seldom	Once in Awhile	Always	Will Consider
1. I initiate contact between employees.	☐	☐	☐	☐
2. I actively seek employee input.	☐	☐	☐	☐
3. I have a secret suggestion program, to encourage the "shy guy."	☐	☐	☐	☐
4. I let employees offer their opinions first—that way, I don't encourage yes-men.	☐	☐	☐	☐
5. I schedule regular meetings for employees and let them brainstorm—without a manager present—on a set agenda.	☐	☐	☐	☐
6. I acknowledge my own problems and limitations and encourage my subordinates to help me improve.	☐	☐	☐	☐
7. I initiate one-on-one contact with my employees.	☐	☐	☐	☐
8. I initiate contact in a nonthreatening way in a nonthreatening place at a nonthreatening time.	☐	☐	☐	☐
9. I assign responses ("Please try to come up with at least four alternative ideas or solutions to this problem for our Friday meeting.").	☐	☐	☐	☐
10. I request assistance from employees in a personal way.	☐	☐	☐	☐
11. I set "think agendas"—for example, a problem of the week.	☐	☐	☐	☐
12. I schedule regular meetings.	☐	☐	☐	☐
13. I assign employees to be "boss" or "troubleshooter" or "expert" or "devil's advocate" for a day.	☐	☐	☐	☐
14. I maintain my sense of humor and perspective when approaching employees.	☐	☐	☐	☐

Step Seven: Contemplate

Before making work-related changes, do you contemplate or hyperventilate? Enthusiasm is behind every success, but it is no substitute for up-front analysis.

Contemplate the following:

	Seldom	Once in Awhile	Always	Will Consider
1. I ask employees for their response to proposed program changes.	☐	☐	☐	☐
2. I thoroughly analyze new ideas.	☐	☐	☐	☐
3. I research suggestions until I have the whole story (e.g., I consult staff, outside experts, reference books, trade publications, others who have instituted a similar change).	☐	☐	☐	☐
4. I examine the worst-case scenario and try to lessen the odds of it happening.	☐	☐	☐	☐
5. I don't burn my bridges.	☐	☐	☐	☐
6. I formulate ideas with the help of employees, encouraging them to "own" the ideas and help make them work.	☐	☐	☐	☐
7. I use idea salesmanship—help employees buy into change.	☐	☐	☐	☐
8. I document how the idea will (or should) benefit employees.	☐	☐	☐	☐
9. I try to lower the risk factors inherent in change.	☐	☐	☐	☐
10. I take change slowly whenever possible.	☐	☐	☐	☐
11. I try not to exceed my employees' comfort level.	☐	☐	☐	☐
12. I admit to myself that there is always room for improvement and I always make room for it.	☐	☐	☐	☐
13. I try to see things through my employees' perspectives.	☐	☐	☐	☐
14. I try to control the amount and presentation of preliminary or premature information.	☐	☐	☐	☐

Step Eight: **Delegate**

To a truly effective manager, delegation means getting things done without getting things to do. Give your workers interesting and challenging tasks—plus the authority, responsibility, and accountability to go with it—and you'll have interested and challenged workers. They'll also be there when you need them.

Do you dabble in delegation? Let's see.

	Seldom	Once in Awhile	Always	Will Consider
1. I make every employee the boss of something.	☐	☐	☐	☐
2. When I make an employee responsible for something, I let other people know it so that they can offer support and assistance.	☐	☐	☐	☐
3. I show faith in an employee's ability to handle the delegated task.	☐	☐	☐	☐
4. I ask subordinates what new tasks they would like.	☐	☐	☐	☐
5. Within time limits, I give employees permission to formally resign from delegated tasks.	☐	☐	☐	☐
6. My employees must answer to each other on their delegated tasks.	☐	☐	☐	☐
7. I encourage old employees to mentor new recruits.	☐	☐	☐	☐
8. I encourage employees to join company committees.	☐	☐	☐	☐
9. I allow hard-working employees to fail without recriminations.	☐	☐	☐	☐
10. I check periodically with employees to offer assistance, BUT I don't continually look over their shoulders.	☐	☐	☐	☐
11. I recognize that delegation requires the cooperation of two people—the "delegator" and the "delegatee."	☐	☐	☐	☐
12. I give high visibility and a title (lead worker in charge of...) to an employee who accepts a new responsibility or job.	☐	☐	☐	☐

SUMMARY

Working to achieve high morale is not a moral issue. It's an issue of dollars and "sense."

Let's go back to the eight steps and note how they help stamp out excessive absenteeism.

STEP ONE   EMULATE

Workers don't do as you say, they do as you do. If you treat absenteeism—yours and theirs—as important, so will they.

STEP TWO   APPRECIATE

People want to be where they feel wanted. Appreciate workers and their value will appreciate.

STEP THREE   INGRATIATE

Your relationship with your employees will make them either want to stay or want to stay away.

STEP FOUR   STIMULATE

Boredom isn't at the root of all absentee problems, but it helps sow the seeds of discontent.

STEP FIVE   INTEGRATE

An employee who feels like a team player seldom skips practice.

STEP SIX   INITIATE

People like to be where the action is. A better absentee record is a common action reaction.

STEP SEVEN   CONTEMPLATE

The best absentee problem is one that has been circumvented through pragmatic planning.

STEP EIGHT   DELEGATE

Nobody wants to miss their own parade!

If you use a majority of these "ate" steps you won't just be a member of the morale majority—you'll be in the elite minority of top managers.

PART 5

NOT BY ACCIDENT

INTRODUCTION

Remember the 80/20 rule?

Most business situations are ruled by the 80/20 rule: 20 percent of the people (inventory, customers, production line, whatever) cause 80 percent of the problems.

The good news about safety is that the 80/20 rule doesn't apply. The bad news is that the numbers are even worse. Ninety percent of all safety problems are caused by something that gets about ten percent of all safety scrutiny.

There's good news in that bad news. On-the-job accidents are a serious source of off-the-job absenteeism. According to the Bureau of Labor Statistics, work injuries and illnesses are on the rise. Six million were reported in 1987, and 6.4 million in 1988. There were 3300 workplace deaths. Managers who can help reverse that statistic are crucial to business profitability.

Ironically, experts blame employee attitude—something that managers can influence—for 90 percent of all accidents. You don't have to be a safety expert to have a safe office or plant. You only have to be an effective "attitude manager."

Here's how.

PREVENT ACCIDENTS NINE WAYS!

THE OUNCE OF PREVENTION

The components of accident prevention, in descending order of importance, are

- Employee attitude

- Participatory management

- Meaningful supervision and counseling

- Job training

- Personnel assignments

- Job analysis

- Inspection (of personnel, equipment, plant, procedures, etc.)

- Routine maintenance

- Appropriate use of space

ACCIDENT CAUSES: THE DIRTY DOZEN

Most accidents occur on the job because

	Not in My Company	Well ...
1. Employees operate equipment without authority or training.	☐	☐
2. Employees don't take precautions to protect fellow workers—they fail to secure equipment, or to warn others of problems.	☐	☐
3. Employees break the equipment's ''speed limit.''	☐	☐
4. Employees circumvent safety checks (for example, they remove safety shields).	☐	☐
5. Employees use inappropriate equipment or tools.	☐	☐
6. Employees use equipment or tools in a careless manner.	☐	☐
7. Employees use their hands when they should use a tool.	☐	☐
8. Employees use an unsafe or unstable posture or position.	☐	☐
9. Employees think of shortcuts to established safe procedures (e.g., they unload a truck by tossing—rather than handing—boxes to coworkers).	☐	☐
10. Employees use unsafe equipment (e.g., equipment that is shimmying on the plant floor).	☐	☐
11. Employees distract other people.	☐	☐
12. Employees forget or refuse to use safety equipment.	☐	☐

Note that the focus is attitudinal, not technical. The Dirty Dozen apply to offices as well as factories.

Most of the Dirty Dozen are attitude problems. Attitude problems are absentee problems. That's why attitude problems are your problem.

THE SAFETY FOUR

For a better safety record, apply the Safety Four:

STEP ONE: Identify potential safety problems:

           Employee hazards—psychological
           Employee hazards—physical
           Mechanical hazards
           Environmental hazards

STEP TWO: Analyze each potential problem until you understand its source.

STEP THREE: Find a solution.

STEP FOUR: Put the solution to work—before the problem puts your employees out of work.

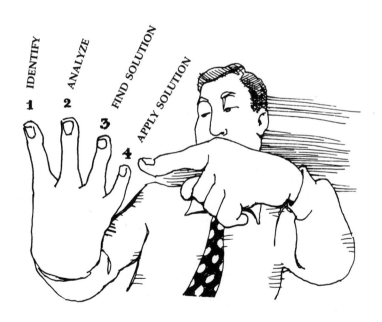

SAFETY FIRST: EMPLOYEE ATTITUDE

There can be no attitude latitude. Employees must be as concerned about safety as you are.

Employees typically behave in dangerous ways because

- they don't know how to do the job correctly and safely.

- they don't realize their actions are risky.

- the safe way is also the inconvenient or uncomfortable way.

- they are in a hurry.

Occasionally, an employee behaves in dangerous ways because he has physical limitations (e.g., a worker with bad eyesight may not see warning signs). If this is the case, you don't have a safety problem. You have a personnel problem. The employee needs to be reassigned.

The remedy for a "bad attitude" is safety awareness. Forget the pat posters or snappy slogans. We're talking safety awareness, *graphic style*.

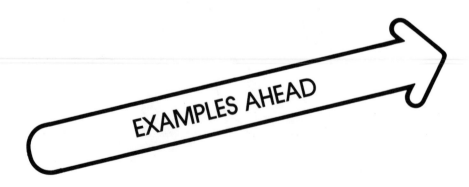

EXAMPLES AHEAD

SAFETY FIRST: TWO EXAMPLES

Example #1:

An employee was killed when he tried to retrieve a small handtool from underneath some heavy equipment. He hadn't bothered to turn the equipment off first.

The company, which had run countless campaigns to stop this kind of careless casualty, had a yellow human outline painted around where the employee died. There have been no similar accidents in that plant in the last 27 years.

Example #2:

Years ago, New York Central Railroad managers wanted employees to wear goggles, but their edicts were met with resistance. The managers decided to show employees what losing their eyesight would mean.

Blindfolded employees were given matches and cigarettes, a toothbrush and toothpaste, a brown (flat) and black (round) shoelace, and two different fabric pieces (one brown, one black). They were told to light a cigarette, brush their teeth, and match the color of the fabric with shoes—all by feel.

Most employees felt pretty foolish when they burnt their fingers, slopped toothpaste every place, and turned out to be "colorblind."

Employees began to appreciate their sight—and goggles that protected it.

SAFETY FIRST: EMPLOYEE PARTICIPATION

Employee participation has less to do with workers than it has to do with management. To improve employee attitudes, managers must allow—not to mention encourage!—subordinates to take an active part in running the business. Participation is the working antonym of alienation.

Your participation summation:

	Yes	No (but will start on it)
1. We have a locked suggestion box and the CEO has the only key. This makes sure that good but controversial ideas do not die prematurely (at the hand of a first line supervisor...).	☐	☐
2. We have a rotating "Safety Supervisor of the Week" schedule for employees.	☐	☐
3. We reward "centers of safety"—individuals, departments, and facilities that have good work records.	☐	☐
4. Safety is a common subject in the office or on the shop floor, at meetings, performance appraisals, and promotion interviews, in the company newsletter, or on the bulletin board.	☐	☐
5. We ask for safety input.	☐	☐
6. We listen to safety input.	☐	☐
7. We recognize that numbers 5 and 6 above are not the same thing.	☐	☐
8. Workers help design safety procedures and training programs.	☐	☐
9. Workers, not managers, sign off or approve apparatus, inspections, and routine maintenance.	☐	☐
10. There are numerous workers on the Safety committee. Their committee clout is equal to management's.	☐	☐
11. We have an open-door policy.	☐	☐
12. We make individual workers responsible for safety within a specific area.	☐	☐
13. We work to gain workers' cooperation.	☐	☐

SAFETY FIRST: THE LITTLE THINGS

Employee attitudes and participation are the major factors affecting on-the-job accidents. But the little things can also prevent some big problems. For example:

PROPER JOB PLACEMENT

According to Dr. Flanders Dunbar, an accidental expert, a public utility company reduced its accident rate by 80 percent—simply by reassigning accident-prone workers to other jobs!

Make sure that workers are physically and mentally suited for their jobs. The lack of manual dexterity or acute vision, for example, can lead to serious industrial accidents. Don't turn a would-be-good elsewhere worker into a good-for-nothing (except worker's comp) employee.

JOB SAFETY ANALYSIS

This is a simple three-step process:

1. Identify how a job should be done.

2. Investigate how the job is being done.

3. Reconcile the two.

THE INSPECTOR GENERAL

Every few weeks, take on the role of inspector general and stroll through the facility. Keep an eye out for both major and minor problems. Create a checklist. It should include both long- and short-term items. For example, stay alert for:

- Narrow, congested corridors or aisles

- Poor traffic patterns

- Overpopulated work areas and crowded workers

- Careless stacking of inventory or supplies

- Unevenly worn floors

- Inconvenient, uncomfortable, or unsafe placement of machines

- Unsafe railings

- Temporary ''band aid'' approaches to situations and problems

- Unsafe treatment of small handtools

- Momentary problems ''I just set that box in the aisle for a minute while I . . .''

- Doors or ventilators full of dust

Don't think of these things as ''accidents waiting to happen.'' Think of them as negligence waiting to be corrected.

Be a Space Cadet

Don't spaceout—learn everything you can about the proper use of office or factory space. For example, how many office workers can safely work in your given space? Is there enough space for important supplies? (Consider the frustration factor of having to walk hundreds of feet to a vital file cabinet.) Can color facilitate your space case? (For example, painting a fluorescent pink behind your fire extinguisher makes a missing canister much more noticeable.)

Little things can mean a lot, particularly when they add a lot of accident-based absenteeism to your lot in life.

SUMMARY

We're back to the 80/20 rule.

What you need to remember about job safety is this:

Whether you're in charge of an office or a factory, on-the-job accidents are an expensive charge against your departmental profits. Help employees develop a positive work attitude, participate in safety issues, and keep track of the little things.

Then you won't need to worry about the 80/20 numbers game. Because your department will have a #1 safety record.

"I USED TO WORK IN FINE CHINA"

PART **6**

THE CASE STUDIES

CASES THIS WAY

K.I.S.S.

The following case studies document how real-world companies have attacked their absentee problems. No, strike that. Not just how they attacked the problems—how they attacked *and won*.

Note how basic and blunt many of these programs are. K.I.S.S.—Keep It Simple Supervisor!—is still the best business policy.

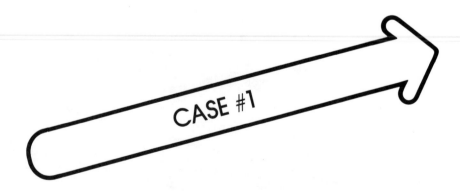

CASE #1

Case #1
The Feedback Factor

The Facts

One department in the University of Illinois at Chicago had a healthy level of absentee use (45.9 sick-pay hours per person per year). A similar section had sickening absentee abuse (59.9 hours). The two groups were being combined.

The Problem

How could managers decrease area absenteeism without instituting a universal crackdown?

The Solution

Managers designed a feedback program of positive, informational letters. Employees in the bottom 10 percent of sick-leave users were sent Letter A (see page 52). Employees in the top 10 percent were sent Letter B.

Managers then let the Hawthorne Effect take effect. What is the Hawthorne effect? When managers pay attention to employees, they will improve.

The Results

Over a span of six years, absentee rates in the less-than-perfect department dropped from 59.9 hours per employee per year to 44.0—a decrease of over 25 percent. The university's savings in that sixth year were estimated to be $500,000.

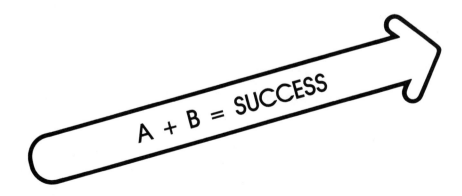

A + B = SUCCESS

CASE STUDY #1 (Continued)

LETTER A

TO:

FROM:

I would like to express my appreciation to you for your excellent employment record during the last year. Our analysis of sick-leave records indicates that you used significantly less sick time than the average campus employee.

On behalf of the campus administration, I would like to thank you for your dedication to your job.

LETTER B

TO:

FROM:

An analysis of sick-leave usage during last year indicates that you used more sick time than the average campus employee. This situation is of great concern because both your welfare and the important work you perform for the university are of great interest to us.

While you are not expected to report to work when you are too ill to perform your job, we urge you to exercise good judgment. We know of some employees who have abused their sick-time benefits and, because they used all of their sick time, were forced to use their vacation time or go into no-pay status when they became truly sick.

On behalf of the University Administration, I hope that this new year will find you in better health.

Case #2
Recognize the Regiment

The Facts

The Maid Bess Corporation had an absentee rate of over 6 percent. This cost the company approximately $700,000 annually in overhead, overtime, and lost sales. This amount would have been substantially higher if Bess Maid had a paid sick-leave program. Maid Bess pays on a piecework basis.

The Problem

Punitive measures, such as less pay, weren't enough to curb excessive absenteeism. Turnover rates (as high as 70 percent in one factory) suggested low morale. Would a positive program have positive results?

The Solution (See page 54 for specifics)

Maid Bess tried different approaches in different facilities:

- A Pay-for-Progress Program
- The Recognition Rationale
- Lavish Lotteries
- Unfaltering Feedback

The Results

- A pay-for-progress program cut the first factory's absenteeism rate from 6.35 to 6.04. This 4.9 percent reduction was statistically insignificant.

- A recognition rationale slashed the second factory's absenteeism rate from 7.56 to 6.04, a 36.9 percent improvement. Maid Bess saved $58,000 in direct labor alone.

- Lavish Lotteries seemed to raise the third factory's absentee rate from 5.59 to 6.11; but the 9.3 percent increase was statistically insignificant.

- Unfaltering feedback reduced the fourth factory's absenteeism rate from 6.33 to 6.09. The 3.8 percent reduction was statistically insignificant.

NOTE: Pay-for-progress, lotteries, and feedback *can* be effective. They just weren't effective here—proof positive that no absentee program can be all things to all people.

CASE STUDY #2 (Continued)

The Solution (Explained)

The Pay-for-Progress Program

- Employees with no absences after one year received $50.

- Employees with one or two absences got $25.

- Employees received no midyear feedback regarding bonus eligibility.

The Recognition Rationale

- Employees who missed no more than one day in the prior quarter received a congratulatory card from the manager.

- Employees with two or fewer absences per year were given a piece of custom-designed, engraved jewelry.

Lavish Lotteries

- One lottery prize (approximate value $200) was given away each quarter.

- Employees with perfect attendance had their name entered twice in the drawing.

- Employees with one absence had their name entered once.

Unfaltering Feedback

- Absentee feedback forms which summarized each employee's year-to-date absence record were distributed with paychecks once a month.

- The forms were informational only and contained no value judgments or program propaganda.

Case #3
Measure the Mayhem

The Facts

Sandvik AB in Sweden had 25 percent absenteeism. That's right, 25 percent. Actually, that isn't as bad as it sounds. Swedish industry has a historically high absentee rate. That 25 percent was in line with local competitors. However, it was nearly double what it had been 25 years before.

The Problem

Sandvik didn't understand its absentee problem. It didn't know if the 25 percent absentee rate was unnecessarily high.

The Solution

Sandvik took a three-prong approach:

1. *Gather The Facts.*

   Sandvik now has a quarterly absenteeism report that is distributed to all production managers.

   Sandvik also started a permanent Absenteeism Committee which consists of three workers and three production managers. It is their job to identify, quantify, and rectify the absentee problem.

2. *Divide And Conquer.*

   Sandvik found that it had *two* absentee rates:

   • The institutional rate (12.9 percent, mandated for national holidays, etc.). This rate was outside the company's control and could not be change.

   • The influenceable rate (14.2 percent). *This the company could reduce.*

3. *Take Action.*

   With help from managers and employees, Sandvik identified and took measures that would help reduce the influenceable absences (see the next page).

The Results

Overall, Sandvik has reduced its influenceable absentee rate from 14.2 to 13.2 percent. Sandvik's Step 3, cut influenceable absenteeism in one department by 65 percent!

CASE STUDY #3 (Continued)

The Sandvik Steps for Influencing Absenteeism

The following ideas were generated during personnel interviews with both foremen and workers. In order, it was determined there was a need to:

1. Improve manager-employee communications.

2. Address and redress employee complaints, such as uncomfortable work environment, or unfair pay differentials.

3. Make sure that managers contact employees after the first day's absence.

4. Make sure that health department employees maintain daily contact with workers during prolonged absences.

5. Provide additional employee orientation.

6. Provide more comprehensive training on new equipment.

"ME? INFLUENCE OUR ABSENTEE PROBLEM?"

Case #4
Looking Well

The Facts

On any given day, one in four Strux Corporation employees exercised some form of absenteeism—late arrivals, early leaves, or no-shows.

The Problem

The company's traditional "absentee entitlement" program discouraged attendance. Sick pay encouraged unnecessary sick leave, and this sick focus forced managers to develop a monitoring mentality.

The Solution

Strux abandoned its traditional structure for a positive payback scheme. Now on-the-job workers (rather than off-the-job-shirkers) receive the leave, and the bonuses.

The Results

Absenteeism is down 83 percent. Nearly 15 percent of Strux employees now have perfect attendance records.

STRATEGY–NEXT PAGE

THE STRUX STRATEGY

1. Strux has no automatic paid vacation or sick leave. These benefits have to be earned.

2. Employees with perfect attendance for a month earn $5 incentive pay and credit toward their annual bonus.

3. Annual bonuses are based on the number of months with perfect attendance:

   • Employees who have worked at Strux for less than five years receive a half-day's pay for every no-miss month.

   • Employees with five or more years of employment get double that.

4. Employees with three consecutive months of perfect attendance earn one day off with pay.

5. Employees with a year of perfect attendance receive five days off and a $200 savings bond.

Case #5
To Everyone's Benefit

The Facts

General Motors' ''controllable'' absentee rate was around 11 percent. Each percentage point pared GM's corporated coffers by approximately $100 million. A study suggested that the company's current labor agreement—particularly its generous benefit program—was a significant source of problems.

The Problem

How could General Motors get tough on absenteeism without making things tougher between management and the strong United Auto Workers union?

The Solution

A new GM-UAW contract (see page 60) was negotiated that tied benefits to hours worked. GM profited from lower absenteeism. Workers gained a more predictable (translation: less stressful) work environment.

> NOTE: This original agreement was amended two years later to include a $500 bonus for workers who maintained a perfect attendance record.

The Results

Controllable absenteeism fell company-wide from 11 to 9 percent. General Motors is saving an estimated $200 million a year.

Some divisions, however, are doing even better. GM's Delco Remy division saw absenteeism decline by nearly 50 percent!

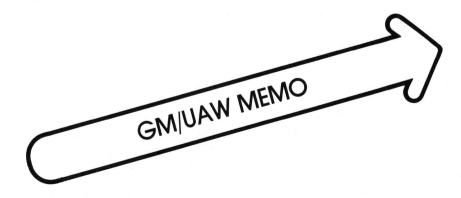

GM/UAW MEMO

CASE #5 (Continued)

The General Motors/UAW Memorandum of Understanding

In discussions of the mutual problem of absenteeism, the parties recognized the basic principle that benefits are generated, earned and funded by regular employment. Accordingly, a major factor in determining an employee's entitlement to these benefits should be regular attendance. In addition, the parties recognized that a small number of employees are absent from the workplace a vastly disproportionate number of days. Moreover, it was apparent that many of these employees have become adept at securing maximum benefits entitlement while at the same time protecting their seniority and avoiding disciplinary measures.

To address these factors, GM and UAW agreed to a Procedure for Benefit Entitlement for Employees with Irregular Attendance. Under this Procedure, employees who experience controllable absences of 20 percent or more of available hours during an agreed upon base period will have their attendance rate calculated as a percent and, therefore, for the next six (6) months, the employee's entitlement to National Agreement benefits will be calculated by using this percentage as a multiplier. The National Agreement benefits that will be so calculated are as follow:

- Holidays

- Vacation Pay

- Paid Absence Allowance

- Bereavement Pay

- Jury Duty

In addition, for the next six (6) months, the employee's work schedule will be forty (40) hours multiplied by the employee's percentage of attendance rate. The benefits that will be so impacted are as follows:

- Sickness and Accident Benefits

- Regular Supplemental Unemployment Benefits and Short Work Week Benefits

In addition, the employee's eligibility during the next six (6) months for the Profit Sharing Plan will be calculated by using this percentage as a multiplier.

A listing of all employees at each facility with a controllable absence rate of 20 percent or more—calculated in the following manner—will be generated:

Controllable absences

Less disciplinary layoffs

Less informal leaves

Divided by available hours

Equals controllable absence rate (%)

To facilitate a smooth introduction of the Procedure, a listing of employees will be compiled using data from October 1, 1981, through March 31, 1982, and those employees with a 20 percent or more controllable absence rate will be counseled regarding their rate of attendance and the future applicability of the Procedure.

Using data beginning April 1, 1982, through September 30, 1982, a 20%-or-more listing will be compiled by the Corporation.

Designated Management/Union officials will revise the list by removing candidates who have experienced major illnesses or injuries such as heart attacks, strokes, major surgery, etc.

Put employee on notice:

- Effective October 1, 1982, joint counseling efforts will be made to help employee correct attendance.

- During the first 6 month period that an employee is covered by the Procedure, the Corporation will counsel the employee in lieu of exercising its right to discipline for attendance-related infractions.

- The controllable absence rate (%) established for the employee during a six month period will be used to determine benefits entitlement for the next 6 months.

CASE #5 CONTINUED

CASE #5 (Continued)

When 20%-or-more are compiled, an additional identification of employees with a 15% to 20% controllable absence rate will also be made and the employees on this list will be jointly advised of the potential for their inclusion in the Procedure should their attendance decline.

At each 6 month interval thereafter (April 1 and October 1) a new 20%-or-more list will be established.

The intent of this Procedure is to address employees who experience the worst attendance levels in the Corporation. However, it is not intended that employees who experience legitimate serious, major injuries or illnesses or employees who, over a span of time, have had excellent attendance records and experience a series of unforeseen or unexpected circumstances be adversely affected. In this regard, while not subject to the Grievance Procedure, problems with the removal of a candidate from the list, or with deductions made in the case of an individual where circumstances subsequently indicate that such deductions were inappropriate, may be discussed between the local designed Management-Union officials in an effort to resolve the problem.

Case #6
Fiscally Fit

The Facts

The General Electric Company in Cincinnati had an average absentee rate of 8.93 days per year per employee.

The Problem

It is generally accepted that employee fitness and recreation programs reduce absenteeism, improve job satisfaction, reduce stress, and improve health.* Would a fitness, recreation, or combination plan be a cost-effective solution to GE's absentee problem?

The Solution

GE gave employees easy access to professionally managed and staffed fitness and recreation programs. The company promoted—but did not coerce—program use.

The Results

Employees who did not participate in the recreation or fitness program had an average absentee record of 8.93 days per year. Workers who participated in the recreation program had an average of 5.28 days, while fitness fans ran around 4.95 days. Employees who participated in both programs averaged 4.83 days.

If the numbers held for GE's 4000 Cincinnati employees, the company would:

- Save $2,874,784 if all employees participated in the recreation program

- Save $3,117,440 if all employees participated in the fitness program

- Save $3,131,212 if all employees participated in both programs.

*For an excellent book on how to implement a wellness program, consider ordering *Wellness in the Workplace* using the form in the back of this book.

CASE #6 (Continued)

General Electric's Plan for Health and Wealth

The Fitness Program

GE's fitness center is run by a professional staff and open to all employees. The well-fit facility contains equipment such as weight machines, rowing machines, exercise bicycles, and treadmills. The professional staff also offers programs in such areas as nutrition, weight training, and stress management.

The Recreation Program

GE's recreation program is run by the General Electric Employee Activity Association. This program is also professionally managed and open to all employees. GEEAA sponsors bowling, golf, softball, volleyball, tennis, and other sports. Educational, social, and cultural programs—such as computer science, painting, and woodshop—are also available.

Case #7
Through No Fault of Their Own

The Facts

A midsize Louisville, Kentucky, cabinet manufacturing company had excessive absenteeism. Thirty-one percent of all employees had nine or more absences, partial absences, or markedly late arrivals (A/PA/LA) every year.

The Problem

A traditional absentee program did not address the company's three main absence abscesses:

- One-day "attitudinal" absences were a day-to-day difficulty.

- Case-by-case discretionary discipline helped employees build a case for system inequity.

- Bogus backup-slips from sympathetic doctors, for example, was being used to justify absences and avoid discipline.

Could a nontraditional absentee program do the job?

The Solution

The firm instituted a no-fault absentee plan. Individual absences were no longer weighed and measured. Absences were simply measured, and if the employee had way too many, he or she was terminated (see page 66).

The Results

- The number of employees with nine or more A/PA/LAs a year dropped by 79 percent.

- The number of employees with six to eight A/PA/LAs fell by 40 percent.

- The number of employees with three to five A/PA/LAs slid by 27 percent.

- The number of employees with zero to two A/PA/LAs increased by 36 percent.

CASE #7 (Continued)

The Fault Line

As a direct result of excessive absenteeism and tardiness, disciplinary action may be required. It will be based on frequency of occurrences in accordance with the following policy:

- Absenteeism will be defined as being absent from work on any scheduled work day, even though the employee has reported said absence to his supervisor.

- Each period of consecutive absence will be recorded as "one occurrence" regardless of the number of days missed.

- Tardiness will be defined as reporting to work within 10 minutes of the scheduled starting time. One occasion of tardiness will be charged as one-quarter of an absence occurrence.

- Employees who report to work late, as provided for in the reporting regulations, or who leave before the end of the shift (with management's permission) will be charged with one-half of an absence occurrence for either of these occurrences.

- Employees who are absent without calling in will be charged with two occurrences of absence for that occasion.

- Absence due to funeral leave, military obligation, jury duty or union business (all as defined in the labor contract) and further, including hospital confinement and work-incurred injury, will not be recorded as an occurrence of absence for purposes of disciplinary action.

- For each calendar month of perfect attendance, an employee with an absentee record will have one occurrence deducted from the absentee record.

- Absence records will be maintained for a consecutive 12-month period, starting with the employee's first occurrence of absence. All absence records and warning slips that are one year old or older shall not be considered for purposes of disciplinary action under this policy.

THE FAULT LINE (Continued)

- Corrective discipline will be administered according to the following:

  — Three occurrences, or points, within a 12-month period: Verbal warning

  — Five occurrences, or points, within a 12-month period: Written warning

  — Seven occurrences, or points, within a 12-month period: Second written warning

  — Twelve occurrences, or points, within a 12-month period: Discharge.

The above policy is in addition to action that may be taken when cumulative time lost from work for any reason substantially reduces the employee's services to the company.

ADDITIONAL INFORMATION: SHOULD YOU BE AT FAULT?

You know where you are now in terms of an absentee policy. Should you be at fault or at no-fault? There are several important points to ponder:

- In a no-fault system, the control of—and responsibility for—absenteeism goes to the workers. If they are out too many times they end up out the door. There is no salvation via excused absences or management leniency. Are you willing to give up the power of parole?

- No-fault systems are roughest on one-day, attitudinal absences. A one-day Monday absence receives the same penalty point as a 40-hour flu. The system protects the legitimate, rejects the inconsiderate.

  Be aware, however, that this "damned if you do, damned if you do more" approach may encourage employees to stretch a one-day dalliance into a full-blown attitude adjustment week.

- Equity is a structural part of the no-fault system. What constitutes an absence, and what constitutes the response, are set forth in the constitution of the program.

  Do managers want this equitable straightjacket? Will they want to make exceptions for long-term employees, highly productive employees, or popular employees? Particularly if the 12th absence is obviously a "legitimate" one?

  Workers, too, may express concern over the fairness of a policy that doesn't distinguish a day at the doctor's from a day at the ballgame.

- Absence-oriented union grievances tend to decrease under no-fault systems. Arbiters tend to rule in favor of no-fault plans because they are objective and equitable, they feature progressive discipline and automatic exceptions (such as jury duty), and they offer the opportunity for redemption. So no-fault systems tend to help managers take care of their business relationships.

  This doesn't mean, however, that unions like no-fault programs. Unions may fault a no-fault plan if they feel it is part of a give-back package (for example, losing hard-won "it's-their-right" sick leave).

Case #8
The Pro and Con Program

The Facts

A midwest nonprofit employment and training agency was experiencing sick-leave shock: $41,000 in sick-leave costs, with absenteeism averaging 53 hours per employee per year.

The Problem

Excessive attitudinal absences were causing the organization to pay sick leave for well-"off" employees.

The Solution

The organization adopted a well-pay plan that had incentives for attendance and disincentives for unwarranted or suspicious absenteeism.

The Results

The first year of the new program resulted in stunning statistics:

- Absenteeism dropped 46 percent.

- The average sick leave per employee fell from 53 hours to 31.

- The organization paid 55 percent less in sick leave.

The Pro and Con Procedures

This two-tier program is the perfect example of the K.I.S.S. approach—Keep It Simple Supervisor.

The Program

1. Employees with perfect attendance over a given four-week period will receive a bonus (four hours' pay).

2. There will be no sick-leave pay for the first eight hours of absence in any one occurrence.

There, wasn't that simple? Best of all it worked like a charm!

CONCLUSION

Absenteeism can be a terrible problem. Any business that has 15 percent of its employees out at any one time will almost certainly compromise its profits, productivity, and performance. Left unchecked, absenteeism will not improve. It will only get worse.

This book has given you several tools to attack absenteeism. Your blueprint for action is simple. First, recognize that a problem exists but can be mitigated. Next, analyze the root causes of individual/company-wide absenteeism. Then consider alternative solutions and communicate your plan. To insure you are on the right track, measure your results, give positive reinforcement and get program feedback. In short, construct a program and then make it work.

The key points to remember:

- **An absentee problem is a morale problem.**

  Follow the eight steps to a healthy "morale majority." Emulate the desired behavior. Demonstrate your appreciation for employees. Ingratiate yourself via fairness, consistency, and consideration. Integrate with - rather than separate from - your work team. Stimulate subordinates. Ingratiate yourself by adopting teamwork as your game plan. Contemplate employee needs and feelings. Initiate worker participation. In short, be an uplifting addition to your division.

- **An absentee problem is an organizational problem.**

  Too many organizational structures tolerate - and maybe even promote excessive absenteeism. Make employees talk to you when they call in sick. Tie benefits to hours worked. Use progressive disciplinary schedules. Pay attention to chronic absentee abusers. You have to get tough on absenteeism. If you don't, absentee costs will be tough on you.

- **An absentee problem is a safety problem.**

  On-the-job accidents create off-the-job workers. Identify potential psychological, physical, mechanical and environmental safety hazards. Analyze each hazard and find its solution. Implement each solution. A supervisor who cares about his workers cares about their safety.

- **An absentee problem is a complex problem.**

  There is no perfect generic absentee plan. Workers and jobs differ. Companies and their organizational cultures differ. The root causes of absenteeism differ. These differences require different managerial tactics. However, there is one perfect absentee plan *for your company*. You'll find it when you identify individual/corporate specifics and design a plan of strategy to match.

Absenteeism is also YOUR problem. And thanks to the techniques outlined in this book, it's a problem you can solve. Good luck!

NOTES

FOR OTHER FIFTY-MINUTE SELF-STUDY BOOKS
SEE ORDER FORM AT THE BACK OF THE BOOK.

NOTES

NOTES

NOTES

FOR OTHER FIFTY-MINUTE SELF-STUDY BOOKS
SEE ORDER FORM AT THE BACK OF THE BOOK.

NOTES

FOR OTHER FIFTY-MINUTE SELF-STUDY BOOKS
SEE ORDER FORM AT THE BACK OF THE BOOK.

NOTES

FOR OTHER FIFTY-MINUTE SELF-STUDY BOOKS
SEE ORDER FORM AT THE BACK OF THE BOOK.

THE FIFTY-MINUTE SERIES

Quantity	Title	Code #	Price	Amount
	MANAGEMENT TRAINING			
	Self-Managing Teams	000-0	$7.95	
	Delegating For Results	008-6	$7.95	
	Successful Negotiation—Revised	09-2	$7.95	
	Increasing Employee Productivity	010-8	$7.95	
	Personal Performance Contracts—Revised	12-2	$7.95	
	Team Building—Revised	16-5	$7.95	
	Effective Meeting Skills	33-5	$7.95	
	An Honest Day's Work: Motivating Employees To Excel	39-4	$7.95	
	Managing Disagreement Constructively	41-6	$7.95	
	Training Managers To Train	43-2	$7.95	
	The Fifty-Minute Supervisor—Revised	58-0	$7.95	
	Leadership Skills For Women	62-9	$7.95	
	Systematic Problem Solving & Decision Making	63-7	$7.95	
	Coaching & Counseling	68-8	$7.95	
	Ethics In Business	69-6	$7.95	
	Understanding Organizational Change	71-8	$7.95	
	Project Management	75-0	$7.95	
	Risk Taking	76-9	$7.95	
	Managing Organizational Change	80-7	$7.95	
	Working Together In A Multi-Cultural Organization	85-8	$7.95	
	Selecting a Consultant	87-4	$7.95	
	PERSONNEL MANAGEMENT			
	Your First Thirty Days: A Professional Image in a New Job	003-5	$7.95	
	Office Management	005-1	$7.95	
	Attacking Absentism	042-6	$7.95	
	Men and Women: Partners at Work	009-4	$7.95	
	Effective Performance Appraisals—Revised	11-4	$7.95	
	Quality Interviewing—Revised	13-0	$7.95	
	Personal Counseling	14-9	$7.95	
	New Employee Orientation	46-7	$7.95	
	Professional Excellence For Secretaries	52-1	$7.95	
	Guide To Affirmative Action	54-8	$7.95	
	Writing A Human Resources Manual	70-X	$7.95	
	Winning at Human Relations	86-6	$7.95	
	WELLNESS			
	Mental Fitness	15-7	$7.95	
	Wellness in the Workplace	020-5	$7.95	
	Personal Wellness	021-3	$7.95	
	Preventing Job Burnout	23-8	$7.95	

Quantity	Title	Code #	Price	Amount
	WELLNESS (CONTINUED)			
	Job Performance and Chemical Dependency	27-0	$7.95	
	Overcoming Anxiety	029-9	$7.95	
	Productivity at the Workstation	041-8	$7.95	
	COMMUNICATIONS			
	Technical Writing	004-3	$7.95	
	Giving and Receiving Criticism	023-X	$7.95	
	Effective Presentation Skills	24-6	$7.95	
	Better Business Writing—Revised	25-4	$7.95	
	The Business Of Listening	34-3	$7.95	
	Writing Fitness	35-1	$7.95	
	The Art Of Communicating	45-9	$7.95	
	Technical Presentation Skills	55-6	$7.95	
	Making Humor Work	61-0	$7.95	
	Visual Aids In Business	77-7	$7.95	
	Speed-Reading In Business	78-5	$7.95	
	Publicity Power	82-3	$7.95	
	SELF-MANAGEMENT			
	Attitude: Your Most Priceless Possession-Revised	011-6	$7.95	
	Personal Time Management	22-X	$7.95	
	Successful Self-Management	26-2	$7.95	
	Business Etiquette	032-9	$7.95	
	Balancing Home And Career—Revised	035-3	$7.95	
	Developing Positive Assertiveness	38-6	$7.95	
	Time Management And The Telephone	53-X	$7.95	
	Memory Skills In Business	56-4	$7.95	
	Developing Self-Esteem	66-1	$7.95	
	Creativity In Business	67-X	$7.95	
	Managing Personal Change	74-2	$7.95	
	Stop Procrastinating: Get To Work!	88-2	$7.95	
	CUSTOMER SERVICE/SALES TRAINING			
	Sales Training Basics—Revised	02-5	$7.95	
	Restaurant Server's Guide—Revised	08-4	$7.95	
	Telephone Courtesy And Customer Service	18-1	$7.95	
	Effective Sales Management	031-0	$7.95	
	Professional Selling	42-4	$7.95	
	Customer Satisfaction	57-2	$7.95	
	Telemarketing Basics	60-2	$7.95	
	Calming Upset Customers	65-3	$7.95	
	Quality At Work	72-6	$7.95	
	Managing Quality Customer Service	83-1	$7.95	
	Quality Customer Service—Revised	95-5	$7.95	
	SMALL BUSINESS AND FINANCIAL PLANNING			
	Becoming A Consultant	006-X	$7.95	
	Basic Business Financial Analysis	022-1	$7.95	
	Effective Collection Techniques	034-5	$7.95	
	Marketing Your Consulting Or Professional Services	40-8	$7.95	

THE FIFTY-MINUTE SERIES (Continued)

Quantity	Title	Code #	Price	Amount
	SMALL BUSINESS AND FINANCIAL PLANNING (CONTINUED)			
	Starting Your New Business	44-0	$7.95	
	Personal Financial Fitness—Revised	89-0	$7.95	
	BASIC LEARNING SKILLS			
	Returning To Learning: Getting A G.E.D.	002-7	$7.95	
	Study Skills Strategies—Revised	05-X	$7.95	
	Basic Business Math	024-8	$7.95	
	Becoming An Effective Tutor	028-0	$7.95	
	CAREER PLANNING			
	Career Discovery	07-6	$7.95	
	Networking Your Way to Success	030-2	$7.95	
	Preparing for Your Interview	033-7	$7.95	
	Plan B: Protecting Your Career	48-3	$7.95	
	I Got the Job!	59-9	$7.95	
	RETIREMENT			
	Personal Financial Fitness—Revised	89-0	$7.95	
	Financial Planning	90-4	$7.95	

OTHER CRISP INC. BOOKS

Quantity	Title	Code #	Price	Amount
	Stepping Up To Supervisor	11-8	$13.95	
	The Unfinished Business Of Living: Helping Aging Parents	19-X	$12.95	
	Managing Performance	23-7	$19.95	
	Be True To Your Future: A Guide To Life Planning	47-5	$13.95	
	Up Your Productivity	49-1	$10.95	
	Comfort Zones: Planning Your Future 2/e	73-4	$13.95	
	Copyediting 2/e	94-7	$18.95	
	Practical Time Management	275-4	$13.95	

VIDEO TITLE*

Quantity	Video Title*	Code #	Preview	Purchase	Amount
	Attitude: Your Most Priceless Possession	012-4	$25.00	$395.00	
	Quality Customer Service	013-2	$25.00	$395.00	
	Team Building	014-2	$25.00	$395.00	
	Job Performance & Chemical Dependency	015-9	$25.00	$395.00	
	Better Business Writing	016-7	$25.00	$395.00	
	Creativity in Business	036-1	$25.00	$395.00	
	Honest Day's Work	037-X	$25.00	$395.00	
	Calming Upset Customers	040-X	$25.00	$395.00	
	Balancing Home and Career	048-5	$25.00	$395.00	
	Mental Fitness	049-3	$25.00	$395.00	

(*Note: All tapes are VHS format. Video package includes five books and a Leader's Guide.)

THE FIFTY-MINUTE SERIES
(Continued)

	Amount
Total Books	
Less Discount (5 or more different books 20% sampler)	
Total Videos	
Less Discount (purchase of 3 or more videos earn 20%)	
Shipping ($3.50 per video, $.50 per book)	
California Tax (California residents add 7%)	
TOTAL	

☐ Send volume discount information.　　　　　　　　　☐ Please send me a catalog.

☐ Please charge the following credit card　　☐ Mastercard　☐ VISA　☐ AMEX

Account No. _____　Name (as appears on card) _____

Ship to: _____　　　Bill to: _____

_____　　　　　　　_____

_____　　　　　　　_____

_____　　　　　　　_____

Phone number: _____　P.O. # _____

All orders except those with a P.O.# must be prepaid.
For more information Call (415) 949-4888 or FAX (415) 949-1610.

BUSINESS REPLY
FIRST CLASS　　　　PERMIT NO. 884　　　LOS ALTOS, CA

POSTAGE WILL BE PAID BY ADDRESSEE

Crisp Publications, Inc.
95 First Street
Los Altos, CA 94022

NO POSTAGE
NECESSARY
IF MAILED
IN THE
UNITED STATES

5510